A RAINFOREST
FOOD CHAIN

A RAINFOREST FOOD CHAIN

ODYSSEYS

A. D. TARBOX

CREATIVE EDUCATION·CREATIVE PAPERBACKS

Published by Creative Education and Creative Paperbacks
P.O. Box 227, Mankato, Minnesota 56002
Creative Education and Creative Paperbacks
are imprints of The Creative Company
www.thecreativecompany.us

Design and production by Blue Design
Art direction by Rita Marshall
Printed in the United States of America

Photographs by Corbis (Tom Brakefield, Fridmar Damm/zefa,
Michael & Patricia Fogden, Kevin Schafer, Kennan Ward), Getty
Images (Tui De Roy, Gerry Ellis, Michael & Patricia Fogden,
David Hiser, Minden Pictures, Mark Moffett, Nacivet, Pete
Oxford, Carsten Peter, Walter Pfisterer, Roy Toft, Steve Winter/
National Geographic, Art Wolfe, Norbert Wu)

Library of Congress Cataloging-in-Publication Data
Tarbox, A. D. (Angelique D.)
A rainforest food chain / A. D. Tarbox.
p. cm. — (Odysseys in nature)
Summary: A look at a common food chain in a South
American rainforest, introducing the cacao tree that starts the
chain, the jaguar that sits atop the chain, and various animals
in between.
Includes bibliographical references and index.
ISBN 978-1-60818-543-6 (hardcover)
ISBN 978-1-62832-144-9 (pbk)
1. Rainforest ecology—South America—Juvenile literature. 2.
Food chains (Ecology)—Juvenile literature.

QH541.5.R27T37 2015
577.34—dc23   2014038232

CCSS: RI.8.1, 2, 3, 4; RI.9-10.1, 2, 3, 4; RI.11-12.1, 2, 3, 4

First Edition HC 9 8 7 6 5 4 3 2 1
First Edition PBK 9 8 7 6 5 4 3 2 1

Cover: A jaguar
Page 2: A waterfall in Costa Rica's rainforest
Pages 4–5: A poison dart frog
Page 6: Amazon rainforest

CONTENTS

Introduction 9

Cacao: The Chocolate Tree 12

Bright Bird 17

Leafcutter Ant: Fungus Gardener 23

Fanged Fish 25

Deadly Beauty 33

Silky Anteater: Super Tongue 37

Endangered Ape 41

Boa Constrictor: Big Squeezer 48

Bloodthirsty Biter 61

Jaguar: Lord of the Jungle 63

Selected Bibliography 76

Glossary 77

Index 80

Introduction

Abird swoops through the sky. In the depths of the sea, a whale dives. A wolf runs for miles across a snow-covered plain. They fly, swim, and travel in search of food. Animals spend most of their time looking for a plant or animal to eat, which will nourish them, provide energy, or help their offspring survive. A food chain shows what living things in an area eat. Plants, called producers, are the first link

OPPOSITE: The green-winged macaw, also known as the red-and-green macaw, is a huge parrot that slowly flies through the rainforest in search of fruits, seeds, and nuts.

on a food chain. Consumers, or animals that eat plants or other animals, make up the other links. The higher an animal is on the food chain, the less energy it receives from eating the animal below it. This is why there are more plants than plant eaters, and even fewer top consumers. Most animals eat more than one kind of plant or animal. Food webs show all of the possible food chains within a wildlife community.

The world's tropical rainforests are found near the equator on the continents of North America, South

America, Africa, Asia, and Australia. Tropical rainforests are home to more kinds of plants and animals than any other biome. Unlike other kinds of forests, no single tree species dominates in a rainforest. Located on the North American continent, Central America's rainforests are packed with trees that tower to heights of 180 feet (54.9 m), shading the ground like giant umbrellas. As many as 900 different trees can be found within a Central American rainforest, along with thousands of different kinds of plants. As amazing as a rainforest's plant diversity is, equally impressive is its variety of animals, many of which have adapted to nest, climb, jump, or fly in the upper layers of the forest. These plants and animals make up numerous food chains, including one that begins with a cacao tree and ends with a brawny cat.

Cacao: The Chocolate Tree

Rainforests around the world
have different plants and animals,
but what all rainforests have in
common is climate. Because
of their location near the
equator, there is little difference
between their summer and
winter temperatures. The daily
temperature range is often greater
than the seasonal range, with a
difference of perhaps 10 °F (5.6 °C)

between the afternoon and night. It rains a lot in the forest—80 to 400 inches (203–1,016 cm) a year—and the average daytime temperature is 77 °F (25 °C). The rain does not fall evenly throughout the year, but even during the drier months of December through May, at least several inches of rain fall per month. Often, the rain comes at night. Humidity, or the amount of moisture in the air, is always high in a rainforest. During the day, the humidity level is usually 60 to 80 percent, and at night, it is even higher.

Because of the great amount of rainfall and the amazing diversity of plants, many people assume that rainforest soil must be the best in the world. In fact, the opposite is true.

The constant rain washes away **nutrients** and leaves the soil claylike. Instead of the black and dark brown dirt that makes up the fertile soils found on the North American prairies, rainforest soils are closer to red or yellow and contain few nutrients. Trees and plants have adapted to living in the rainforest's infertile soil by conserving and recycling the nutrients they are able to get. Most rainforest plants have shallow roots to absorb decaying leaves, feces, or dead animals, which are quickly broken down by fungi and bacteria.

The North American continent's tropical rainforests are concentrated in the region known as Central America. In this region grows the cacao tree, which has been cultivated as a crop for more than 2,000 years. The cacao tree is part of a tree family called *theobroma*, which means "food for the gods." The Aztec and Mayan Indians made drinks and pasta from the tree's pods, or fruit, and even used the pods as money. After the Spanish conquered

Bright Bird

The colorful quetzal has a green body that is about the length of a football. Males of this brilliant bird species have 38-inch (96.5 cm) tail feathers that make them appear much larger. When the Mayans ruled Central America from A.D. 317 to 650, the quetzal's feathers were treasured like gold. Death was the penalty for anyone caught killing the bird, and only certain people were allowed to trap the quetzal, pluck its feathers, and let it go. The quetzal is known to feed on a variety of rainforest fruits, but its favorite is the avocado. It even plans when it will mate around the ripening of at least 15 different kinds of avocados in the rainforest. The quetzal's bright coloring acts like camouflage amid the bright rainforest trees, and its long tail can be mistaken for ferns. Birds called toucans and weasel-like animals called tayras prey on young quetzals, and today, the quetzal is endangered because much of its habitat in the Central American Cloud Forests (the mountainous regions of the rainforest) has been destroyed.

the Indians in the 1500s, cacao became a profitable crop for Spain. Even as late as the 1800s, the plant's seeds remained a form of currency in many parts of Central and South America.

The cacao tree grows well in the shade of other rainforest trees and requires constant humidity and rainfall of at least four inches (10.2 cm) a month. It also requires year-round temperatures averaging between 68 and 74 °F (20 to 23.3 °C). Most cacao trees reach heights of 26 feet (7.9 m) and grow best at lower rainforest elevations, although some farmers today cultivate cacaos as high as 3,280 feet (1,000 m) up in mountainous areas.

Monkeys, parrots, and other small animals help spread the cacao tree's range. They are attracted to the cacao's fruit, which grows from the tree's limbs or trunk. Cacao fruits look like orange footballs when they are ripe. Yanking a cacao fruit from its slim, flimsy stem, a monkey pounds the pod against a tree to crack it open. Inside the pod are rows of seeds surrounded by white pulp. The pulp is sugary sweet, but the seeds are sour and powdery. Monkeys spit the seeds out as they move through the rainforest chewing the sweet pulp. The cacao tree has been spread through the rainforest in this way for millions of years.

n the last few thousand years, farmers have helped to spread cacao seeds, too. The bitter seeds spit out by monkeys today make up a multimillion-dollar industry. Cacao seeds, also called cocoa beans, are the main ingredient of chocolate, considered by many people to be the finest flavor ever discovered. One cacao tree produces enough seeds to make more than 70 chocolate bars. Thanks to the global demand for chocolate, cacao trees are grown by the thousands on huge plantations in Central America and other tropical regions of the world.

Cacao trees are deciduous and grow new leaves up to four times a year. Depending on the amount of sunlight the tree needs, it raises and lowers its leaves to maximize photosynthesis. The older sections of the tree grow tiny flowers that are pollinated all year long by tiny insects. Four months after pollination, cacao fruits develop and ripen. As soon as the pods turn their orange color, they are pecked at by birds, yanked loose by monkeys, or gnawed open by rainforest squirrels. Although these animals crave the tree's fruit, there is a tiny, six-legged animal that marches up and down the tree searching not for cacao fruit but for leaves.

Leafcutter Ant: Fungus Gardener

The ground looks as if it is moving when leafcutter ants trek through the rainforest. These rainforest ants are about the length of a human fingernail, although the ant queen is much larger—about the size of a sixth-grader's thumb. Leafcutter ants have no bones but rather an exoskeleton, or hard outer covering, that gives them protection and shape. Their exoskeleton is a

23

yellowish-red color and is made up of a material called chitin, much like the shells of shrimp.

Like all insects, leafcutter ants have three body sections: head, thorax, and abdomen. From their mouth area extend mandibles, which the ants use like hands to fight, pull, or grab on to things. The parts they use to chew food are called the maxillae. The thorax area of the ant's body contains most of its muscles. Ants have six legs, and only the queen and the drones—a few special male ants meant to breed with a queen—have wings. Inside the abdomen are the ant's organs and blood that is clear like water.

Leafcutter ants live in underground colonies, or nests, of up to 8 million. New colonies are started from May to as late as December, when a leafcutter ant queen takes off into the air about 30 minutes before sunrise for several

Fanged Fish

Whether piranhas are as small as eight inches (20.3 cm) or as long as two feet (61 cm), these freshwater South American fish routinely kill animals much larger than themselves. Piranhas' jaws and razor-sharp teeth can cut through bone, and the jutting lower jaw of their bulldog-like faces allows them to take large chunks out of prey. Piranhas sometimes swim in schools of 1,000 or more, and good eyesight enables them to distinguish between 20 colors, which helps them spot animals in the water. They can also smell blood from great distances. They usually eat other fish, but when a large animal, such as a capybara, comes to the water for a drink, piranhas may swarm, taking walnut-sized bites out of the animal's legs. The capybara collapses, and the piranhas attack the animal's sides and internal organs. Within minutes, the capybara is reduced to bones. However, the piranha is not invulnerable to predation in the rainforest's rivers and streams. Caimans, small relatives of crocodiles that sometimes fall prey to jaguars, often eat piranhas.

nights in a row. Drones from many colonies also take off around the same time. The queens and drones release pheromones, or special chemicals, that send signals to attract each other. After the queen mates with several drones, she finds a spot on the ground and digs a small chamber. The drones die after mating.

To start her new colony, the queen carries in her mouth a special fungus that has a symbiotic relationship with all leafcutter ants. The fungus is the main food of young and adult leafcutter ants, but they will also eat leaf

Silky Anteater: Super Tongue

As it sits high in a tree, the gold fur of a silky anteater gives it the appearance of a piece of fruit. It is the smallest of the three anteater species found in the rainforest, about the size of a bag of potato chips. Its tail is 6 to 12 inches (15.2–30.5 cm) long, almost as long as its body, and it has a narrow snout and an extremely far-reaching tongue, which it sticks into the nests of its favorite prey: ants. A silky

OPPOSITE: One of the silky anteater's defining features is its sharp claws. If threatened, the anteater will stand on its hind legs and hold its front claws up in a striking position.

anteater weighs only about half a pound (227 g), making it a featherweight in comparison to its biggest cousin, the 66-pound (29.9 kg) giant anteater that roams the same rainforests.

The silky anteater has a prehensile tail, which means that it can wrap and bend the tail, and even hang from it if necessary. It uses its tail for balance and as an emergency brake to clutch the tree in case it slips. The anteater's rear feet are flexible, like human hands, and it has sharp front claws. It has adapted to an arboreal,

Silky anteaters tend to spend their time alone except when raising young. Females have large territories and usually don't tolerate other females in their area.

or tree-living, lifestyle. In fact, silky anteaters rarely descend to the rainforest floor, spending almost all of their sleeping and waking hours in trees, especially ceiba trees.

Silky anteaters seem to prefer ceiba trees because the pods on the tree are a similar color to the anteaters' fur and therefore offer good camouflage from predators such as the harpy eagle. Silky anteaters tend to spend their time alone except when raising young. Females have large territories and usually don't tolerate other females in their area. However, a male has an even larger territory (up to 25 acres, or 10.1 ha) and can go where he pleases. Usually, a male has three females in his territory, and he may mate with all of them.

A female silky anteater usually gives birth to one cub after a five-month pregnancy. The father typically does not stick around for long but may offer the young anteater regurgitated, or partially digested, ants to eat. For about eight hours every night, the mother anteater leaves her cub unattended as she hunts. While the cub's mother is out doing her evening hunting, the

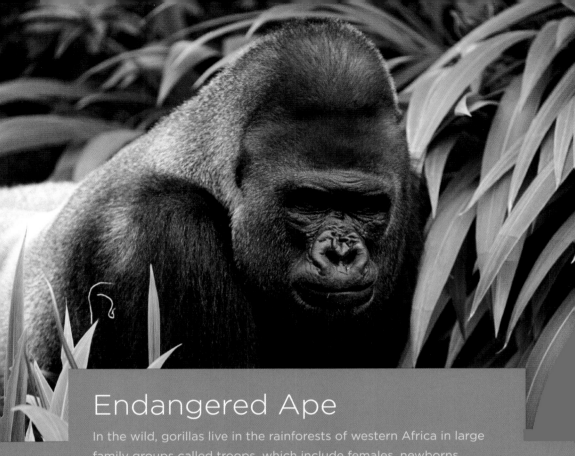

Endangered Ape

In the wild, gorillas live in the rainforests of western Africa in large family groups called troops, which include females, newborns, and juveniles. The leader of the troop is a dominant male called a silverback. Young males stay with their troop until they are around 10 years old, at which time the hairs on their back begin to turn silver, and they leave to start their own families. Every morning, the troop sets off to forage amid the wealth of food the rainforest has to offer, such as grubs, wild celery, and tree fungus. Gorillas eat soil, too, which provides them with calcium and iron. When threatened, male gorillas stand and beat their chest and sometimes charge their enemy, whether it be a human or a leopard attempting to eat their young. They can weigh up to 400 pounds (181 kg) and are incredibly strong. Gorillas are endangered because of overhunting and rainforest habitat loss. Despite improved law enforcement, poachers still illegally kill gorillas and sell their meat and body parts, such as hands, as souvenirs.

To get at ant colonies that live in the tree, silky anteaters use their front claws to slice the bark and then stick their tongue inside as if licking a bowl clean.

young silky anteater searches for ants and termites to eat along the branch where it was left. Every day at dawn, when the mother returns, she carries her cub on her tail or back to a new tree in her territory, where they will spend the day resting. This new tree is also where she will begin her hunt in the evening. When the young silky anteater is about half-grown, it will leave its mother and travel until it has left her home range in order to find a territory of its own. Silky anteaters usually live up to three years.

Silky anteaters eat up to 8,000 ants during their evening hunts. Sometimes also consuming termites, silky anteaters visit about 20 trees a night, licking ants off leaves and eating the ants they find under the bark. To get at ant colonies that live in the tree, silky anteaters use their front claws to slice the bark and then stick their tongue inside as if licking a bowl clean. But they don't wipe out an entire ant colony. Instead, they take less than 1 percent of the ants available and then move on to find another group. They also do not spend much time feeding at a single site. The reason for this may be that soldier ants soon begin to attack the anteaters, and it becomes too painful for them to stay.

Silky anteaters sometimes will consume as many as 18 different ant species in a night, visiting many

After eating thousands of ants during its night of foraging, a silky anteater finds a comfortable, high branch from which to hang and rest until its next feeding time.

trees until dawn. A silky anteater often comes across leafcutter ants while the ants are out scouting and collecting leaves in the evening. Clasping a branch with its hind feet and prehensile tail, the silky anteater strikes with its long, sticky tongue, bringing the ants into its mouth. After eating some leafcutter ants at one spot, the anteater moves to another section of the tree to repeat the process.

Leafcutter ants have ways to defend themselves from foraging anteaters. When an ant is under attack, it sends out an alarm pheromone that calls soldier leafcutter ants to come to its aid. Using their mandibles, the soldiers pinch and stab the silky anteater in an effort to defend the workers. Eventually, the anteater moves on to eat other ants. As it does so, though, it needs to be careful, for hanging nearby may be a hungry predator waiting to put the death squeeze on an anteater.

Boa Constrictor: Big Squeezer

Boa constrictors are big snakes that range in color from tan with black markings to leafy green with thin bands of white. They are as much at home in rainforest trees as they are slinking around the forest floor or going underground into the homes of animals such as the agouti, a kind of rodent. Boa constrictors average 8 feet (2.4 m) in length, with the longest one

The boa constrictor's body is covered by smooth scales that look like they've been painted with varnish.

ever recorded measuring 18 feet (5.5 m) long. The snakes are found from Mexico all the way to South America and when full-grown are one of the forest's top predators.

The boa constrictor's body is covered by smooth scales that look like they've been painted with varnish. Many boas also have bands of red, black, and yellow scales at the end of their tail, which may be an adaptation meant to warn potential predators away, as the colors mimic the poisonous coral snake. Many scientists believe that snakes evolved from lizards because many snakes, including the boa, have remnants of lizard-like parts on their body. Near their rear vent, the part of boas' bodies where they release waste, the snakes have tiny back limbs

OPPOSITE Many boas, such as the emerald tree boa, have a leafy green coloration that blends into the rainforest foliage. The big snakes use stealth rather than speed to hunt.

with claws. They also have pelvic bones and two lungs, whereas most snakes have one.

Unlike other kinds of snakes, female boa constrictors do not lay eggs but instead give birth to live young. Neither the father nor the mother snake takes care of the newborn babies. It is as if the young boas come into the world already programmed in how to hunt and survive. As many as 60 boas are born at one time, each about 20 inches (50.3 cm) long. The majority of the young boas will not reach adulthood, becoming prey to jungle cats

Some species of snakes can live as long as 50 years in captivity, but the oldest boa on record reached 40 years.

such as the ocelot and other carnivores such as the tayra. But those that do live to adulthood have few enemies. Some species of snakes can live as long as 50 years in captivity, but the oldest boa on record reached 40 years.

Boa constrictors are nocturnal hunters, and because they are cold-blooded, they have to find shade if they are too hot or bask in sunlight to warm up if they are too cold. Boas that have recently eaten prefer to digest their food where the temperature is higher. Boa constrictors are excellent climbers and are able to get up into trees using a motion called rectilinear progress, in which their belly scales lift out and grip the tree's bark. They use the same method to travel on the ground. Whether in the trees or on the ground, the boa is a slow mover, usually traveling at speeds of about one mile (1.6 km) per hour.

Because boa constrictors are so slow, they do not catch their prey by pursuit. Instead, they rely on the art of ambush. The first stage of their hunting involves finding prey. Boas may move from underground burrows to high branches in their search for food. Capable of very quick lunges, boas are skilled at snatching bats and birds from the air as they fly by, and sometimes the

Although long portrayed as evil, frightening creatures in books and movies, most wild boas pose no threat to humans, pursuing only prey of swallowing size.

snakes will stay in the same tree for a month if the place is visited often by prey animals.

While in a tree, a boa will remain very still, curled around a branch, flicking its tongue to smell the air. A boa's eyesight is poor, but it has heat-sensing organs around its mouth that alert it when an animal is near. If the boa senses that a silky anteater has come to its tree, the snake watches with patience as the animal, distracted by its search for ants, moves from branch to branch. Finally, when the anteater comes close enough, the boa strikes, its mouth opened wide. The boa is not venomous but relies on its sharp teeth to impale and hold the silky anteater long enough for it to wrap its body around the animal like a noose, squeezing and suffocating it. The silky anteater tries to use its sharp front claws to defend itself, but the big snake ties it like a prisoner so that the anteater cannot lift its legs. As the anteater tries to gasp for air, the boa tightens its hold. Soon, the anteater cannot breathe at all.

The boa has flexible jaw joints that allow it to open its mouth wider than the size of its prey. Once the silky anteater stops moving, the boa begins swallowing it head-first. The snake's muscles contract and, like a conveyor belt, push the anteater down into the boa's stomach. A silky anteater meal will sustain a grown boa for several days. As the slow-moving boa slithers off in search of a place to rest and digest its meal, the rainforest's top predator, the biggest cat in the Western Hemisphere, is on the prowl.

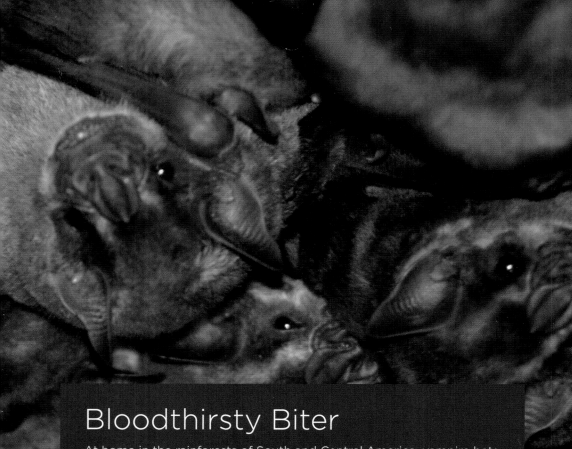

Bloodthirsty Biter

At home in the rainforests of South and Central America, vampire bats have been portrayed in folklore for centuries as horrible bloodsuckers of the night. In reality, vampire bats do not suck blood; they lick it. Using echolocation, vampire bats are able to locate and determine the size of potential prey at night. In their nose are heat sensors that help them find veins close to the surface of their victim's skin. With great precision, a vampire bat uses its scalpel-like teeth to create a tiny cut on an animal such as a sleeping monkey or horse, or even a human. The victim's wound starts to bleed, and anticoagulant substances from the bat's saliva keep the blood flowing until the bat is done feeding. Vampire bats will lap about three teaspoons (14.8 ml) of blood. The blood meal is high in protein and provides all the nourishment vampire bats need. The spectral bat, also called the false vampire bat, with its 32-inch (81.3 cm) wingspan, is one of the largest bats in the world and likes to eat vampire bats.

Due to their huge population and almost nonstop activity, leafcutter ants make a serious impact on the rainforest, cutting up almost 20 percent of all leaves.

juice and flower nectar (a sweet liquid made by plants). Inside the chamber, the queen immediately starts trying to grow a fungal garden with her own feces. Almost 90 percent of new queens die during this stage because they cannot provide the right conditions for the fungus to grow. If the fungus does grow, the new queen will lay up to 1,000 eggs a day.

ost of the eggs hatch about 35 days later as **sterile** female ants that will serve as workers and soldiers. Ants called media workers go into the

rainforest and collect leaves on which the fungus grows. Media workers can carry leaves that weigh more than 30 times as much as they do across the rainforest floor. To put this in perspective, it would be like an average 7th-grader carrying a 3,000-pound (1,361 kg) truck over his or her head and hiking through miles of forests and mountains. However, media workers do not collect and carry just any leaves. The ants are particular, and of all the plants and trees available in the rainforest, they take leaves from only about 80 different species.

The media workers are very careful when they try out new plant material. Often, they will wait several days before deciding to use or reject a new leaf, basing their decision on chemical signals from the fungus. Once a new leaf or part of a leaf has been brought to the colony, other worker ants lick it clean. These leaf-licking ants, also sterile females, are called minima workers. The minima workers chew each leaf, spreading their saliva and dropping their feces across every leaf meant for the fungus. These substances work like fertilizer, providing the perfect combination for the fungus to grow. Large soldier ants protect the media ants during their foraging trips.

Media ants trek through the rainforest 24 hours a day on paths they have cleared. One of the species of rainforest trees from which they take leaves is the cacao tree. Marking a path with a scent that will

Deadly Beauty

Poison dart frogs come in many brilliant colors, including red, green, yellow, and blue. Their **aposematic** coloring is meant to alert **predators** that sickness or death will result if the frogs are eaten. For centuries, Colombian Chocó Indians have captured the frogs for use in hunting, collecting their poison by boiling them or by holding them down with sticks and then rubbing their darts on the frogs' backs and sides. After poisoning their darts, the Indians release the frogs back into the rainforest, where they eventually replenish the poison taken from them. The poisoned darts are deadly, capable of knocking a monkey out of a tree or even killing a jaguar within seconds. Poison dart frogs manufacture their deadly toxins using substances in the rainforest insects they eat, such as certain species of ants, spiders, and centipedes. Even though some poison dart frogs have enough poison to kill 10 people or more, birds such as rufous motmots and fire-bellied snakes can eat them with no ill effects.

help guide them back to their nest, the workers climb the cacao tree and head straight to the leaves. Using their mandibles like scissors, they cut pieces of cacao leaves, sometimes stripping the tree of all its leaves if there are not enough trees in the area. Cacao trees can do nothing to defend themselves against the ants.

Hoisting the leaf parts high above their heads as if carrying a flag, the leafcutter ants trek down the tree and form straight lines as they march back to their nest. Juvenile worker ants, called hitchhiker ants, often ride on top of the cacao leaves and begin the process of cleaning the leaves and preparing them for the fungus. They do their best to fight off threats such as the coffin fly. But threats to leafcutter ants do not always have wings. Leafcutter ants collecting cacao leaves are also vulnerable to a long-tongued beast that may be walking the branches, hunting for a snack.

Jaguar: Lord of the Jungle

With retractable claws as sharp as daggers and teeth that can pierce a turtle shell or crocodile skin, the jaguar is an awesome hunter. Male jaguars, 8.5 feet (2.6 m) long from head to tail, can weigh up to 300 pounds (136 kg). Females are about 25 percent smaller than males. A jaguar's coat color can be all black, but it is usually a golden brown shade with black rosettes, or circular spots, randomly repeated all over its fur.

OPPOSITE: Jaguars are considered a keystone species, meaning they have a very important role in the community of rainforest organisms.

The jaguar prefers to ambush its prey under or in rainforest trees, but it can also be found in the water ...

The jaguar prefers to ambush its prey under or in rainforest trees, but it can also be found in the water waving its tail to lure fish or hunting for turtles and crocodile-like caimans. Its head is large and whiskered, and its jaws are more powerful than those of most large cats. The jaguar is the only big cat that habitually eats **reptiles**, and researchers have theorized that its strong teeth and jaws developed for the purpose of piercing through their hard skin and shells.

Because the jaguar prefers wet habitats near streams and rivers, its tracks are easily found, which has almost led to the great cat's extinction. By 1972, both poaching (illegal hunting) and killings by farmers fearful for their livestock had landed the jaguar on the endangered species list in many parts of North America and earned it near-threatened status from the International Union for the Conservation of Nature. However, the biggest threat to jaguar populations today is the destruction of its habitat. It is estimated that there are only about 15,000 jaguars left in the wild.

For every 39 square miles (101 sq km) of rainforest, there may be 1 jaguar. The jaguar is territorial, but a female's home range often overlaps with a male's. In the rainforest,

The sizes of Central and South America's rainforests were reduced dramatically in the 20th century due to logging, road building, and "slash-and-burn" agriculture.

the jaguar's deep, hoarse-sounding roars can be heard day or night, announcing its territory. Scratch marks, urine, and feces left on trees and paths are all means of communicating with other jaguars, conveying the message that the cat may be ready to mate or warning other cats to stay clear of its home range.

Jaguars mate year round, and after about a three-month pregnancy, a female jaguar usually gives birth to two cubs inside a cave or a place of dense, concealing vegetation. The cubs start to eat the meat of such animals as capybara (the world's largest rodent) around 10 weeks of age. The cubs stay with their mother for up to 18 months, learning to hunt before leaving her to find their own territories. Jaguar fathers do not help with the care of the cubs.

Jaguars are known to eat more than 85 different animals in the rainforest, from monkeys in the trees to peccaries on

Heavily muscled yet very agile, the jaguar is a versatile predator. It is an excellent climber, good leaper, and strong swimmer, and it can hunt effectively day or night.

the ground to catfish in the rivers. They are powerful enough to kill and eat almost anything they come across in their home range. Jaguars hunt by walking slowly through the rainforest, listening for sounds and watching for movement.

They may also climb trees or hide in the shadows of brush, waiting to ambush an animal. The mirror effect of jaguars' eyes gives them better vision in the dark than during the day, but they hunt day or night. Jaguars might spot boa constrictors either in a tree or on the ground.

Clamping its powerful jaws around the boa, [the jaguar] first tries to pierce and crush the snake's skull.

Jaguars are fast runners, but they rarely move at top speed except for a few explosive seconds. After spotting a boa, a jaguar slowly stalks the reptile until it is in range, then it pounces.

Unlike other large cats, which kill their prey by biting the neck, a jaguar attacks the head. Clamping its powerful jaws around the boa, it first tries to pierce and crush the snake's skull. If it is unable to bite the boa's head, it attacks the reptile's long body. Using its enormous paws, the jaguar tries to hold down the writhing snake as its teeth pierce the scaly flesh and bones of the boa. If the boa cannot slither away from the jaguar, it will try to wrap its coils around the large cat to stop the attack. The jaguar's assault continues until the boa stops moving. After the boa is dead, the jaguar drags it to a place with dense vegetation so it can eat in seclusion. Unlike other large cat species, jaguars usually start by eating the head of the animal and work their way down. What the jaguar does not eat it will return to later, sometimes taking several days to finish a meal. It usually will not hunt again until it has finished eating the animal it killed.

The boa in the jaguar's belly is linked to the silky anteater, the leafcutter ant, and the cacao tree in the rainforest food chain. When the jaguar dies, scavengers such as army ants and king vultures will eat their fill. Nutrients from the dead jaguar's body will eventually return to the jungle soil, helping plants such as cacao trees grow, and the rainforest food chain will start again.

Selected Bibliography

Dewey, Jennifer Owings. *Poison Dart Frogs*. Honesdale, Penn.: Boyds Mills Press, 1998.

Fleisher, Paul. *Ants*. Tarrytown, N.Y.: Benchmark Books, 2002.

Forsyth, Adrian. *How Monkeys Make Chocolate: Foods and Medicines from the Rainforest*. Toronto, Ontario: Greey de Pencier Books, 1995.

Janzen, Daniel H., ed. *Costa Rican Natural History*. Chicago: University of Chicago Press, 1983.

Ling, Mary. *The Snake Book*. New York: DK Publishing, 1997.

Lynette, Rachel. *Piranha*. Farmington Hills, Mich.: KidHaven Press, 2004.

Patent, Dorothy Hinshaw. *Quetzal: Sacred Bird of the Cloud Forest*. New York: William Morrow, 1996.

Glossary

adapted   made changes over time—such as growing thicker fur or eating other foods—to survive in an environment

aposematic   describing an animal that has noticeable markings meant to warn other animals that eating it might result in illness or death

bacteria   microscopic, single-celled organisms that can live in the soil or water or inside animals and plants; some bacteria are helpful to their host, but others are harmful

biome   a region of the world that is differentiated from others by its predominant plant life and climate

camouflage   outer colors of an animal that help to disguise or hide it

deciduous   describing a tree that annually sheds its leaves during a certain season

echolocation   the process of locating prey by sound waves that are usually sent from an animal's head and echo back to tell it the location and identification of nearby animals or objects

endangered   at risk of disappearing from Earth permanently; plant and animal species are said to be endangered when they near extinction

foraging	moving around in search of food
fungi	a classification of organisms that do not have chlorophyll (the green coloring of plants) or inside supporting tissues; examples include mushrooms and molds
habitat	the place a plant or animal lives
nutrients	minerals, vitamins, and other substances that provide an organism with what it needs to live, grow, and flourish
photosynthesis	a process by which plants exposed to sunlight are able to make their own food
pollinated	fertilized by the transfer of a powdery dust called pollen from one plant to another
predators	animals that live by killing for their food
reptiles	cold-blooded animals that have a backbone and scaled skin or a hard shell; examples include snakes and turtles
scavengers	live animals that feed on dead animals
species	animals that have similar characteristics and are able to mate with each other
sterile	unable to produce offspring
symbiotic	a relationship in which two different organisms live together and receive benefits from each other

territorial   describing animals that have an
            attachment to a property and mark the
            boundaries of it, usually with feces and
            urine, and often will fight to keep it

tropical   characterized by year-round temperatures
            above 64 °F (17.8 °C) and frequent rainfall

Index

bacteria 14
boa constrictors 48–50, 52–53, 57–59,
    73, 74
    color 48, 49
    constriction 58
    enemies 49, 52
    habitat range 49
    hunting 50, 52, 53
    life span 52
    prey 53, 57–58, 59
    rectilinear progress 52–53
    size 48–49, 50
    young 50, 52
cacao trees 11, 14, 18–19, 21–22, 32, 34,
    35, 74
    fruit 14, 19, 21–22
    human uses for 14, 18, 21
    leaves 21, 22, 32, 34, 35
    seeds 18, 19, 21
    size 18
caimans 25, 64
capybaras 25, 68
ceiba trees 39
fungi 14, 27, 41
gorillas 41
jaguars 25, 33, 63–65, 68, 72–74
    color 63
    communication 68
    cubs 68
    endangered status 65
    hunting 63, 64, 68, 72–73, 74
    prey 64, 68, 72, 73, 74
    reproduction 68
    size 63
    territories 65, 68
leafcutter ants 23–24, 27, 30–32, 34–35,
    46–47, 74
    colonies 24, 27, 31
    defense against anteaters 46–47
    drones 24, 27
    eggs 30
    fungal gardens 27, 30, 31, 32, 35
    leaf cutting 34
    media ants 30–31, 32

    queens 23, 24, 27, 30
    reproduction 24, 27
    size 23
    soldier ants 30, 32, 47
    worker ants 30, 31, 32, 34
monkeys 19, 21, 22, 33, 61, 72
photosynthesis 21
piranhas 25
poison dart frogs 33
quetzals 17
rainforests 11, 12–14, 17, 18, 65
    destruction 17, 65
    plant diversity 11, 13
    rainfall 13, 18
    soil 13–14
    temperatures 12–13, 18
silky anteaters 37–40, 42–43, 46, 47,
    57–58, 59, 74
    cubs 40, 42
    enemies 39
    hunting 40, 42, 43
    life span 42
    reproduction 40
    size 37, 38
    tail 37, 38, 42, 46
    territories 39–40, 42
    tongue 37, 43, 46
spectral bats 61
tayras 17, 52
termites 40, 43
vampire bats 61